Math Flow

Rhymes for junior high math

Cindy Mosley

DEDICATION

To students who love poetry but hate math.
Or
To students who love math but hate poetry.

Who am I kidding?

To junior high math teachers brave enough to incorporate poetry in the math classroom.

CONTENTS

ACKNOWLEDGMENTS

I could think of no other way
To brighten my students' dreary day
Than to add a rhyme to what I say.

C. Mosley

1
POETRY IN MATH

"Maths and poetry are not truths waiting to be discovered at the end of a spreadsheet, but man-made languages that open up our horizons of understanding."
Shirley Dent (2009)

My teacher has found another way
To teach me math
She is using poetry
Can you imagine that?

She has us writing poetry
Using steps from our notes.
We sing to solve problems
And chant the steps we wrote.

2
SUCCESS HAPPENS WHEN

"I can try many times and many ways to understand and solve math problems."

Success may not happen the first time
The second or the third
But if success is your goal
Perseverance is your word.

3
ACHIEVEMENT 101

I forgot to bring a pencil
And I lost my notes in band.
Instead of doing nothing
I simply raised my hand.

Teacher loaned me a pencil
I copied my neighbor's notes
I got more accomplished today
Than I had hoped.

4
NOT YET

"Using words like "yet" and "not yet" is giving kids greater confidence. "
Carol Dweck

"Not Yet" is what we say

When we haven't mastered a skill.

Because if we keep trying

Eventually we will!

5
I DIDN'T GET AN "A"

The world didn't end when I didn't get an "A"
My life wasn't over when I got a "B".
But when I wanted to play in the game
I knew I needed at least a "C".

6
MY MATH TEACHER CALLED

My math teacher called my house today
Not because I did something bad.
He called to give a praise report
To my mom and dad.

Apparently I accomplished something
I hadn't done before.
I discovered a formula
To find the area of the walls minus the door.

He also bragged on me
Saying I did something new.
I figured out how much paint we needed
To paint all the walls blue.

I thought my teacher hated me
That was my mistake.
Because he was very proud
That today I was awake.

7
TRIANGLES & SLOPE

Teacher, teacher, hear my rhyme
How am I supposed to use triangles
To find the slope of a line?

Yes, you said to take the rise and put it over run.
I thought that would be fun.
But the fraction scared me when I was done.

8
I GET TO USE A CALCULATOR!

Using a calculator is really cool
Except it comes the rules.

I can use it for practice
And even on my tests.

But I must never use the calculator
To support the legs of my desk.

9
ALGEBRAIC REPS WRECKED MY REP

I was doing great in math
I had good grades to tell
Until we studied transformations
Then my grades just fell.

Translations were easy.
All they do is slide across the plane.
Their algebraic reps was add or subtract
There's nothing to their game.

Reflections are like a mirror.
They flip left, right, up, or down.
The algebraic reps are simple
The signs just switch around.

Dilations are my favorite
They get big or small.
Their algebraic reps multiply by a scale factor
Image over original of sides or coordinates is all.

Now rotations are tricky.
Because even though they turn
Their algebraic reps
Cause my brain to burn.

I try turning my paper
Following degrees
But when I try to plot the points
My brain always freeze.

Can anyone help me find a way
That I can get this right?
I need to pass the retest today
So I can get my phone back tonight.

10
EQUATION BOXES

I can solve equations
Using inverse steps one at a time.

But when it comes to writing them
I can't keep them in line.

So teacher taught me
To use a special box.

That's when I discovered
I like writing equations a lot.

11
FUNCTIONS ARE MY FAVORITE

Functions are my favorite.
Teachers likes them too.
It didn't take long to learn.
"X" can have only 1 "Y", not two.

There is a vertical line test
For checking up and down
The line can go through only one point
And not loop around.

12
NOT SO TRENDY

Scatterplots are nothing new.
They show data of two kinds.
What makes me frustrated though
Is when I have to extend the lines.

Why can't they just ask something simple?
Like where would the point fit?
Instead they actually want me
To take time to predict.

13
FORMULA CHART, FORMULA CHART

Formula Chart, Formula Chart
What do you say?
I have to find the volume
Of a sphere today.

I also need to find Simple Interest
Compound Interest too
Teacher said you can help me
With all I have to do.

That includes surface area
And the slope of a line.
I can get the answers
When I do what you advise.

Formula Chart, formula chart
What do you say?
I want to get the answers right.
On my test today.

14
REAL NUMBERS ON A LINE

I learned to use number lines
In elementary school.
Now that I'm in junior high
They've turned it into an ordering tool.

Square roots, percents, and integers
Must be converted first to use
As decimals or fractions
And ordered by their values.

If I have a long decimal, I round it first
To the nearest value I see.
I add zeroes if I need to
To make ordering simple for me.

15
SCIENTIFIC NOTATION

Scientific notation is supposed to be easy
It's multiplying a decimal by a power of ten.
But when I have to choose,
I get the wrong answer over and over again.

Teacher told me to think of money
With values between a dollar and ten.
But what about the zeroes
And the exponent?

I guess I have to try something else
Like giving the calculator a try
The setup is simple
Just MODE and S-C-I.

Resources

Dent, Shirley (2009) Final proof that maths and poetry have a special relationship Retrieved 7-18-2017 from
https://www.theguardian.com/books/booksblog/2009/feb/04/maths-poetry-pi-fibonacci

Dweck Carol The Power of Believing that You Can Improve, Retrieved 7-18-2017 from
https://www.ted.com/talks/carol_dweck_the_power_of_believing_that_you_can_improve

ABOUT THE AUTHOR

Cindy Mosley is a junior high math teacher with a passion for reaching the hearts of kids. She is the author of More Than a Math Teacher: A teacher's guide for coaching middle school students to succeed in math. Follow Cindy on Facebook at https://www.facebook.com/cmosleymathcoach/?ref=bookmarks.

Made in United States
North Haven, CT
15 July 2022

21411458R00015